Published by Peterson's Guides in cooperation with the National Association of Trade and Technical Schools, the Office of Student Financial Assistance of the U.S. Department of Education, and the Consumer Information Center of the U.S. General Services Administration.

**Consumer
Information
Center**

National Association of
Trade and Technical Schools

Peterson's Guides

Getting Skilled, Getting Ahead

Your Guide for Choosing a Career and a Private Career School

James R. Myers, Ph.D.
Elizabeth Werner Scott, M.A.

Peterson's Guides

Princeton, New Jersey

Library of Congress Cataloging-in-Publication Data

Myers, James R., 1930–
   Getting skilled, getting ahead : your guide for choosing a career and a
private career school / James R. Myers, Elizabeth Werner Scott.
     p.   cm.
   Bibliography: p.
   ISBN 0-87866-868-3
   1. Vocational guidance—United States—Handbooks, manuals, etc.
  2. Technical institutes—United States—Handbooks, manuals, etc.
  3. Occupational training—United States—Handbooks, manuals, etc.
  4. Personnel service in secondary education—United States—
Handbooks, manuals, etc. I. Scott, Elizabeth Werner, 1946– .
II. Title.
HF5382.5.U5M87   1989
331.7'02'0973—dc 19   89-3066
                                              CIP

Composition and design by Peterson's Guides

Printed in the United States of America

10 9 8 7 6 5 4 3 2

Contents

(continued)

Preface

The unchanging fact about jobs and the future is that both are constantly changing. Everyone will be affected by these changes.

Here are just a few predictions and observations about working and the job market:

- By 1995, more than half of all jobs will require education or technical training beyond high school.
- By the year 2000, an estimated 5 to 15 million manufacturing jobs will require different skills, while an equal number of service jobs will be obsolete.
- By 2000, the major contributors to new job opportunities will be small companies with fewer than 100 employees, yet small companies are the least able to provide remediation and training.
- Workers will change jobs six to seven times during their normal working lives.
- Many technical and office occupations now require postsecondary career training as more employers prefer to hire trained personnel rather than provide training.
- Over 2 million students now attend postsecondary career schools each year.

What do these statements mean as you think about a job for yourself and for your future?

- You will probably have several jobs in your lifetime, and they probably will be different kinds of jobs.
- More and more, employers will only hire workers who already have the required skills.
- Training will be the key to staying in the mainstream of the work force.

- Schools that offer specialized postsecondary training may be your answer to getting skilled and getting ahead.

This guide was written to help you plan for your future. The first chapter talks about jobs and money. This chapter will show you how the job you get can affect many other parts of your life.

Chapter 2 helps you to look at jobs you can do and enjoy doing and lets you know where you can get information and assistance when deciding on a career.

The third chapter introduces you to private career schools and gives you an inside look at what these schools can offer.

Chapters 4 and 5 are road maps to finding out about training opportunities.

The Job Profiles at the back of this book can help you identify some of the occupations for which private career school training is available.

And last but not least, we encourage you to *go for it*. You are the one who has the power and ability to plan your future, to look at your life, and to decide what it takes to *get skilled and get ahead!*

Dr. James R. Myers
Elizabeth Warner Scott

Chapter 1

What's in It for Me?

In this chapter, you will explore the jobs available to skilled and unskilled workers. What opportunities do workers without specific career skills have? What is the earning potential for an unskilled worker? How would having a skilled job change your life? Will you be able to meet your needs and fulfill your goals with the jobs you are qualified for right now?

FOR YOURSELF, TODAY

Getting a job may not seem like a big deal. After all, you probably see "help wanted" signs all the time. It's true that most of these jobs require a high school diploma and some previous experience. Sometimes the hours are bad, but the job helps you to pay for a roof over your head and puts food in your mouth.

But it doesn't take long to realize that there is much more to life than just food and shelter. Think about talks you have had with your friends—what you said you wanted out of life and what your friends are after in their lives. How close are you to getting those things with a low-paying, unskilled job?

Let's take a few minutes to figure out how much it costs to live for a month. Suppose your job pays around $5 per hour, which is realistic for an unskilled job. At $5 per hour full-time, your total pay (before taxes) would be $200 per week, or $867 for 4 1/3 weeks, the average working month. Then we can use the percentages given by the U.S. Department of Labor for an average American family budget to create your own profit and loss statement for a month.

YOUR PROFIT AND LOSS STATEMENT

Income		$867
Expenses		
Food (25%)	Includes *all* fast food lunches	217
Housing (23%)	Includes utilities and maintenance	199
Taxes (20%)	Includes Social Security contributions	173
Transportation (8%)	Includes gas, repairs, and insurance (for your own car)	69
Clothing (7%)	Covers clothes and laundry	61
Medical (5%)	Less than one doctor's visit per month	43
Personal Care (2%)	Includes haircuts	17
	Total Living Expenses	**$779**
Profit (Net Gain)	Includes entertainment, monthly emergencies, and savings	$88

If you made $5 an hour working full-time, you would have $88 a month after expenses. With that money, you could go to the movies and do other fun things. It would also go toward monthly emergencies. You would probably want to save some of this money to be able to afford a nicer place to live or a better car. You would have many uses for this $88.

If these numbers don't seem too bad to you, then spend the next couple of days doing the following:

- Look at apartment rents in the newspaper.
- Decide on the clothes you would like to have and check out the prices.
- Go to the grocery store to buy a week's worth of food, spending no more than $40. Don't eat at a restaurant all week.
- Find out how much it costs to ride the bus per week or how much gas costs to run a car for a week.

Notice that there isn't much left over for savings—savings to buy a car, take a trip, or buy something special for yourself, a friend, or a relative. The opportunities to be really free and independent increase with your ability to make money!

Now that you have your mind on the dollars and cents part of living, let's look at the "what ifs." What if you spent several months or even a year or more training for a career? Let's say you learn a skill that puts you in a job that pays more than unskilled jobs pay. Let's imagine that in this skilled job you earn $6.50 per hour. Your total income for 4 1/3 weeks would now be $1,127 instead of just $867, and your monthly expenses would look like this:

Income	$1,127
Expenses	
Food	282
Housing	259
Taxes	225
Transportation	90
Clothing	79
Medical	56
Personal Care	23
Total Living Expenses	$1,014
Profit	$113

That additional $260 per month you receive in pay because of your training will make your living conditions better. You could treat yourself to special events or buy some fun clothes with some planning on your part. Over a lifetime, a difference of $1.50 in your hourly wage will mean a significant increase in your income. For example, if you made $5 an hour, after forty years you will have earned $416,000. But at $6.50 an hour, you will have made over a half million dollars ($540,800).

These examples are a quick way of answering the question, "What's in it for me to spend my time, money, and energy in a training program?" But a better job and more pay are just part of the answer—today's answer. Looking down the road at job responsibilities and growth after training provides even more to think about.

FOR YOURSELF, TOMORROW

When employers hire someone in a minimum wage job, they expect a day's work for a day's wages. Such work is not usually long-term. If there is less work, employees will be laid off. If the work picks up again and more workers are needed, then there always will be other people around to take the job. People in minimum wage jobs are often treated like spare parts, used only when needed. You may be a great busboy, but your services will no longer be required if business slacks off. Businesses with changing work needs usually hire a lot of unskilled workers.

Another concern with unskilled jobs is the lack of possibilities for advancement. Such work doesn't often involve much training or the chance for development. You may increase your chances to get a better job if there is an opportunity, but most unskilled jobs do not provide such opportunities. You may receive a few dollars' increase from time to time, which can improve the way you live today, but how about tomorrow?

Teaching you skills that will help you to get a better job, make more money, and climb to a level where you are hard to replace in a company is what private career schools are all about. Having marketable skills is a form of security for you!

FOR YOURSELF

"Money isn't everything" is an old saying, but there may be times when you wonder whether it is true. Think about those talks with your friends. What do they want out of life, and how do they feel about what they do for a living?

Maybe you feel that it is enough to find work to put a roof over your head and food on your table. But, in addition to needing a paycheck, most people want and need to feel that they are valuable and that what they do has meaning. Of the 16–17 hours you are awake each day, 10 are usually spent in the business of working—2 hours going and coming from work and 8 hours on the job. The people with whom you work are usually the people with whom you socialize. They are the people who know you and who influence how you feel about yourself. So a job means more than just finding work and making money.

Today, people are demanding more from their jobs—they are looking for careers. Why?

- A career can involve working with interesting things, people, and ideas.

- A career can provide stability and security with a job that you feel will be there tomorrow regardless of changes in the economy.

- A career is a job with a future, allowing you to learn new things so that you can be promoted and earn more money.

- A career job will demand abilities and talents that not everyone has, that you can be proud of having mastered, and that are appreciated by your employers.

You will have reached your first success when you get that new job—the one that requires training. You will have spent money, energy, and time planning for this career change. Your success will be the result of deciding on a goal and following the steps described in this guide. You will have proved to yourself and to others that you can plan for your future.

Chapter 2

Knowing Where You're Going

This chapter is about choosing a career. You will consider your skills, interests, and values and how to match them up with your career options. You will be given advice on how to find the information needed to make a career decision. You will begin to take the practical steps necessary to change your future.

FIRST QUESTIONS

"What do you want to be when you grow up?" is a question that everyone has heard. It suggests that there is a simple answer and that somehow each of us should know exactly what career is right for us. The truth is that there are many careers for each of us. According to labor experts, we will probably change jobs and careers *six to seven times* during our working lives.

Did you know that by the year 2000, there will be as many new jobs that do not exist today as there are current jobs available? So how will all this change your plans?

You may not be able to choose just one career for the rest of your life. The decision you make today to learn the skills you need to get the "right" job is simply the first decision of many that you will have to make in a lifetime. This means that it is very important to first learn how to make decisions about your career goals. This knowledge will give you the tools to begin, to improve, and to change careers as the world of work changes around you.

Although the process for exploring careers is straightforward, it involves a considerable effort. You will need to spend some time looking at yourself, deciding what is important to you, and gathering information on possible careers. After that, you will need to learn where to get training to pursue your chosen career. This may seem like too much work, but think about how much your decision will affect the other parts of your life. It will affect the amount of money you'll earn and how well you'll like your job. It will also influence the environment you live in, the friends you make, and the plans you have for the future. If you consider that in a ten-year span you will spend over 20,000 hours working, you will realize that the time spent deciding on the skills you need and where to get them is really not very great.

CHECKING WITH YOURSELF

Before you can decide what careers you might like, you must look at yourself. You need to decide what's important to you, what interests you, and what abilities you have. As you mature, you will develop a system of personal values. Often what's valued by you is something you do well and, therefore, is something you really enjoy doing. These three important items—values, skills, and interests—will help you select a job that brings you satisfaction and success.

A couple of sample exercises are included to help you understand your skills, interests, and values.

GETTING TO KNOW YOUR OWN SKILLS AND INTERESTS

Now, let's find the pattern of skills that have been most responsible for your past successes and will probably be important to your future successes.

As you think about your successes, remember that not all the things you have accomplished are necessarily successes. Whether something is a success or not depends on your opinion, not on what anyone else thinks or says.

Write down your answers to these questions.

1. What is the first success that comes to your mind? Describe it briefly. What was your age at that time?

   _____

   _____

   _____

2. What parts of your latest job or hobby do you do best and enjoy most?

   _____

   _____

   _____

3. What do you like to do or enjoy most when you are not at school or work? Give two or three examples.

   _____

   _____

   _____

4. What topics have you enjoyed studying on your own? Give two or three examples.

_____

_____

_____

_____

5. Write down briefly as many of your successes as you can. They do not need to be in any particular order. They can come from any time period and any area of your life.

_____

_____

_____

_____

_____

Now review your answers to these questions. What are your interests, and what are your talents? What have you been successful at? Can you see any patterns forming? Note any information that might be important to your career decision.

WORK VALUES

Work values are not right or wrong. Work values are job-related things that are important to the employee. What aspects of a job are important to you?

WORK VALUES EXERCISE

Assess your opinion of the following job conditions.
Mark the box that best describes your feelings.

	Very Important	Somewhat Important	Not Important
Work near your home			
Work within an hour of home			
Work for a small company			
Work for a large company			
Work outdoors			
Work indoors			
Be physically active			
Work at a desk			
Work with others			
Work alone			
Be a part of a team			
Compete with others			
Be given work and directions			
Work independently			
Do same things each day			
Have a variety of tasks			
Be recognized for achievements			
Help others			
Make a good profit			

Look over the values you have marked as very important. These are work needs for you to remember when you are selecting a career.

CHECKING WITH OTHERS

This guide should help you to start thinking about your skills, interests, and values. But this book is just the beginning. There are many other resources available to help you.

This would be a good time to visit a career counselor at your school, at a private career school, or at your state employment job service. You might even plan a visit to the local community college. Counselors can help you to identify your skills, interests, and values at little or no cost. That's their job, and you are the reason they exist.

CHECKING OUT CAREERS

After you have taken time to think about what's right for you, the next step is to find a skilled job that you would like. This is the first of several fact-finding missions you will go on. There is a lot of help available to assist you in completing your mission.

When first looking at careers, you should start with general books that list a number of career fields. You might even begin by reviewing the Job Profiles section in the back of this book. There you will find an alphabetical listing of more than 100 skilled jobs for which private career school training is available. The public library or local school library will be your next stop. The librarian can help you find books to assist you in your career search. The *Occupational Outlook Handbook*, compiled by the U.S. Department of Labor, is a book that can help you. *The Encyclopedia of Careers and Vocational Guidance* is also good. It describes over seventy major industries and job fields and lists hundreds of careers. The *Chronicle Occupational Briefs* also contains useful information. Look over these books and others like them early in your career search.

Each of these books describes an occupation in terms of requirements and responsibilities. These publications discuss physical requirements, the working environment, and necessary training and education. Also included is information on the number of workers in the career field and their average earnings and the national employment outlook for the career.

Once you have found careers that you like and that suit your work needs, look for books that will provide more detailed information. Many professional societies, trade associations, labor unions, business firms, and educational institutions can help you. They will give you career information free or at a low cost.

Don't forget to talk to people in the career fields you are interested in. Speak to your friends, neighbors, or relatives—anybody you think of as successful. Most people like to talk about what they do. Through these conversations, you can get the facts about a career and also find out how these people got their jobs and what aspects of the job they like most. If possible, go to a job site and look at the workers. Watch what they do and how they do it. Check out the equipment and think about whether you would like to do the same kind of work.

A small word of caution is needed here:

- Always check the date of printed information. Some career information gets old quickly. In particular, information about wages changes very fast.

- Always consider the source of the information. Some materials are produced to provide general career data, and other materials are meant to promote a certain career. Promotional materials often provide career information but may not provide you with the whole career story; sometimes, only the best things are listed about the career field.

You will need all the information that you have collected to make your career decision. You should pay special attention to what you would be doing in the job. Also, remember to look carefully at the working conditions. As part of your fact-finding mission, you should consider what might happen to your chosen career in the future.

CHECKING THE FUTURE

As you think about a new career, you must also think about the future of that career. A career as a typesetter in a printing shop may be appealing to you and may pay well, but will there be a demand for skilled workers in this job a few years from now? Current job projections say no.

Growth or decline in the demand for skilled workers in a particular job occurs for several reasons. Technological change is a major factor in the decline of several occupations. Another factor is the shift in the country's economy. The U.S. economy seems to be shifting from goods-producing industries (making products like coal and refrigerators) to service-producing industries (offering such services as health care, education, repair and maintenance, amusement and recreation, transportation, banking, and insurance). This trend is likely to continue.

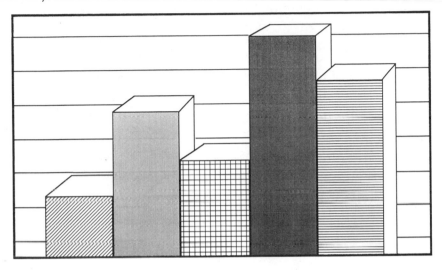

You should look closely at the career you think you like in light of the current and projected changes in the economy. Decline or growth in an industry will affect growth in individual jobs differently depending on the types of jobs the industry uses. Consumer demand can affect several different industries. For example, the rising cost of gasoline created a demand for more fuel-efficient cars, and the automobile industry responded with smaller, lighter-weight cars that give more miles to each gallon of gas. Which industries were affected by this change?

- Iron and steel were used less and therefore the demand decreased for (1) manufactured iron and steel goods, (2) the products used by iron- and coal-mining industries, and (3) the services of industries that supply iron and steel manufacturers.

- Plastic, aluminum, and specialty steel were used more and therefore the demand increased for (1) goods manufactured from these materials; (2) the products used by the plastic, aluminum, and specialty steel industries; and (3) the services of the industries that supply the plastic, aluminum, and specialty steel manufacturers (including mining operations).

Look at the following three tables developed by the U.S. Department of Labor to see what jobs will grow and what jobs seem to be declining. Remember, however, that the fastest-growing fields do not always provide the most jobs. These tables will give you an idea of the type of information you will find in career handbooks. You will need to know how to read the information presented in charts such as these in order to make a well-informed career decision.

THE TWENTY FASTEST-GROWING OCCUPATIONS, 1986–2000

(Ranked by greatest expected percentage increase, not necessarily largest expected job growth)

Occupation	Number of Jobs		
	1986	2000 (projected)	Percentage increase (rounded)
Paralegal personnel	61,000	125,000	104
Medical assistants	132,000	251,000	90
Physical therapists	61,000	115,000	88
Physical and corrective therapy, assistants and aides	36,000	65,000	82
Data processing equipment repairers	69,000	125,000	80
Home health aides	138,000	249,000	80
Podiatrists	13,000	23,000	77
Computer systems analysts, electronic data processing	331,000	582,000	76
Medical records technicians	40,000	70,000	75
Employment interviewers, private or public employment service	75,000	129,000	71
Computer programmers	479,000	813,000	70
Radiologic technologists and technicians	115,000	190,000	65
Dental hygienists	87,000	141,000	63
Dental assistants	155,000	244,000	57
Physician assistants	26,000	41,000	57
Operations and systems researchers	38,000	59,000	54
Occupational therapists	29,000	45,000	52
Peripheral electronic data processing equipment operators	46,000	70,000	51
Data entry keyers, composing	29,000	43,000	51
Optometrists	37,000	55,000	49

Source: U.S. Department of Labor, Bureau of Labor Statistics, 1987.

THE TWENTY FASTEST-GROWING OCCUPATIONS, 1986–2000

(Ranked by greatest expected growth in actual jobs, not necessarily the fastest-growing occupations)

Occupation	Number of Jobs		
	1986	2000 (projected)	Increase
Salespersons, retail	3,579,000	4,780,000	1,201,000
Waiters and waitresses	1,702,000	2,454,000	752,000
Registered nurses	1,406,000	2,018,000	612,000
Janitors and cleaners (including maids and housekeeping cleaners)	2,676,000	3,280,000	604,000
General managers and top executives	2,383,000	2,965,000	582,000
Cashiers	2,165,000	2,740,000	575,000
Truck drivers (light and heavy rigs)	2,211,000	2,736,000	525,000
General office clerks	2,361,000	2,824,000	463,000
Food counter, fountain, and related workers	1,500,000	1,949,000	449,000
Nursing aides, orderlies, and attendants	1,224,000	1,658,000	434,000
Secretaries	3,234,000	3,658,000	424,000
Guards	794,000	1,177,000	383,000
Accountants and auditors	945,000	1,322,000	377,000
Computer programmers	479,000	813,000	334,000
Food preparation workers	949,000	1,273,000	324,000
Teachers, kindergarten and elementary	1,527,000	1,826,000	299,000
Receptionists and information clerks	682,000	964,000	282,000
Computer systems analysts, electronic data processing	331,000	582,000	251,000
Cooks, restaurant	520,000	759,000	239,000
Licensed practical nurses	631,000	869,000	238,000

Source: U.S. Department of Labor, Bureau of Labor Statistics, 1987.

THE TWENTY FASTEST-DECLINING OCCUPATIONS, 1986–2000

(Ranked by greatest expected percentage decline, not necessarily occupations losing the greatest number of jobs)

Occupation	Number of Jobs		
	1986	2000 (projected)	Percentage decrease (rounded)
Electrical and electronic assemblers	249,000	116,000	–54
Electronic semiconductor processors	29,000	14,000	–51
Railroad conductors and yardmasters	29,000	17,000	–41
Railroad brake, signal, and switch operators	42,000	25,000	–40
Gas and petroleum plant and system occupations	31,000	20,000	–34
Industrial truck and tractor operators	426,000	283,000	–34
Shoe sewing–machine operators and tenders	27,000	18,000	–32
Station installers and repairers, telephone	58,000	40,000	–32
Chemical equipment controllers, operators and tenders	73,000	52,000	–30
Chemical plant and system operators	33,000	23,000	–30
Stenographers	178,000	128,000	–28
Farmers	1,182,000	850,000	–28
Statistical clerks	71,000	52,000	–26
Textile draw-out and winding-machine operators and tenders	219,000	164,000	–25
Central office and PBX installers and repairers	74,000	57,000	–23
Farm workers	940,000	750,000	–20
Coil winders, tapers, and finishers	34,000	28,000	–19
Central office operators	42,000	34,000	–18
Directory assistance operators	32,000	27,000	–18
Compositors, typesetters, and arrangers, precision	30,000	25,000	–17

Source: U.S. Department of Labor, Bureau of Labor Statistics, 1987.

SUMMING IT UP

Once you identify your interests, skills, and values and explore some careers, you can set a goal and make your first decision. Here are some questions you should ask yourself:

Is the career goal reasonable in terms of my ability?

Is the career goal realistic in terms of my personality?

Is the career goal realistic in terms of my work habits?

Is the career goal reasonable in terms of available training opportunities?

Consider how much time, money, and desire you have to prepare yourself for a career before you make your selection.

When you can answer yes to all four questions, you are on your way to making what you want to be a reality. You are ready to ask the big questions—the what, where, when, how, and how much—whose answers can start you off toward a new career.

CAREER EXPLORATION CHECKLIST

(Make several copies to compare your options.)

Title of job_____

Additional education/training required_____

_____

How long will it take to acquire the necessary training?_____

_____

How much will training cost?_____

When will I get a job?_____

Entry-level training skills required_____

_____

_____

Summary of job duties_____

_____

_____

Working conditions_____

_____

Entry-level pay_____   Salary range_____

Promotion opportunities_____

_____

Number currently working in the career_____

Projected job openings in the future_____

Opportunities available in my community_____

_____

Personal advantages and disadvantages_____

_____

Chapter 3

Finding the School

How much do you know about private career schools? This chapter introduces you to them. It covers topics such as locating and contacting schools, requesting catalogs, and interpreting catalog information. Chapter 3 hopes to answer the question, "Why should I consider a private career school?"

CHOOSING A PRIVATE CAREER SCHOOL

Selecting the right school—the school that's right for you—is as important as selecting the right career. Schools that specialize in offering career training are called private career schools.

Why select a private career school? Here are some of the reasons so many career schools are good at training people for good-paying, rewarding jobs.

- Because private career schools are privately owned, they are ready to respond to the ever-changing needs of business and industry by developing new courses and making changes in instruction that quickly become part of their programs.

- Private career school teachers work with the needs of each student in mind. (Students can usually work and complete courses at their own pace.) Teachers are selected from business and industry, where they have gained practical experience in their chosen career field. Because of their on-the-job experience, they know industry standards and what skills are required to be successful.

- Private career school programs are usually shorter than those in public schools or private four-year colleges. Only the specific skills required to be successful in a career are taught. The school knows that the sooner the training is completed, the sooner you can start earning a paycheck.

- Private career schools are designed to respond to the needs of individual students. Students with special requirements, including those who may need instruction in spoken English and those with physical handicaps, often find that programs can be tailored to meet special considerations.

- These schools maintain up-to-date equipment. Because the teachers come from business and industry, they know what equipment is necessary for your training.

LOCATING SCHOOLS

Many types of private career schools are located in large cities. Highly specialized schools may be far away from your home. If you are interested in nearby schools, the easiest thing to do is to look in the yellow pages of local phone books under the heading of schools or training. In addition, many schools advertise in newspapers and on radio and TV. Some will mail school materials to your home.

Not all schools advertise in these ways, and you may also want to consider schools outside of your immediate area. If so, you may need to find school directories. Many states have published directories for postsecondary vocational schools.

Your high school counselor or a librarian at a public library can help you find these directories. At the very least, a directory provides the school's name, address, and phone number and information on the training programs offered. The National Association of Trade and Technical Schools (NATTS) publishes a free *Handbook of Private Accredited Trade and Technical Schools*. A copy is easily obtained by writing to:

NATTS
Department GG
P.O. Box 10429
Rockville, Maryland 20850

Don't overlook the obvious when considering schools. Remember to talk with your friends and people working in the career you want to enter. Many students in private career schools heard of their school through someone they knew who graduated and successfully started a new career.

CONTACTING THE SCHOOL

Once you have some names and addresses of private career schools, you will want to contact them for detailed information. If you call the school, you probably will talk to a receptionist first. You will need to tell the receptionist that you are interested in a training program and that you would like to receive a catalog and financial information. (Be ready to give your mailing address and zip code.) The receptionist may handle your call or suggest that you talk to a school official. Sooner or later, a staff official will need to talk with you in person. You may decide to look over the school's catalog and call later for an appointment.

If you choose to write to a school, your request should be brief and to the point. Your letter may be handwritten or typed. Be sure that your address and phone number are very clear. You can use the sample letter that follows to write for information.

Date

School Name
Mailing Address

Dear Sir or Madam:

I found the name of your school in (list where you found the name). I am interested in (list the training program) and would like to receive more information.

I graduated from high school in (year) (or, I last attended school in year). Please send me your school catalog and information on tuition and training costs. My mailing address and phone number are listed below.

Thank you,

Your Name
Mailing Address
Phone Number

EXPECTATIONS

Once you have school catalogs in hand, you are ready to begin your next fact-finding mission. It is at this point that you become a buyer. As a buyer, you should expect certain things from the school you choose.

Private career schools can be expected to provide you with specialized training to get and keep a job in the career that you have selected. Of course, a school can only help you if you are willing to make the effort to finish the program.

You can expect the teachers at the school to know the career field and to be experts at teaching you the skills you will need.

You can expect the school to know what skills are needed and to make those skills a part of your training program. Private career schools are noted for their ability to get the training done and not to spend a lot of your time teaching you things that are not required. They know you want to go to work and to start earning money as soon as possible.

You can expect that the school's staff members have carefully consulted with business and industry on the type of equipment and materials used. Only after knowing what is being used in the field can schools select equipment and materials for training.

You can expect these schools to make changes in what and how they teach when changes take place or are about to take place in the businesses and industries for which they prepare students. Schools should make sure that you receive the training needed to be successful in your career today and tomorrow.

You can expect the private career school to take a personal interest in you. The school will work with you and be your partner, helping you to reach your career goal. After all, without successful students, private career schools could not be successful themselves.

You can expect the private career school to provide individual placement assistance. Unlike colleges and universities, private career schools make job placement a central part of the program. It's as important to them as it is to you that you find a job after graduation.

You can expect the school's staff to be businesslike in responding to all of your questions. Don't be afraid to ask! These professionals are proud of what they do, and they will be glad to talk to you.

WHAT'S IN A CATALOG?

There are many different looks to a career school catalog. Some catalogs contain many pictures; others are very colorful. The catalog offers the school an opportunity to put its best foot forward. But you need to look at *what* the catalog says rather than how it looks. Here are some items that should be in a school catalog and some tips for interpreting the information you will read.

Licensing and Accreditation

Most states require that a school be licensed by the state in order to operate as a private postsecondary educational institution. At the very least, the school should say that it is approved by the state board of education.

In addition, the U.S. Department of Education recognizes certain accrediting agencies that have established standards to improve the quality of education in private career schools.

Why is accreditation important to you? If a catalog says that the school is accredited, then you know that the school

- Truthfully advertises its services
- Clearly sets forth the terms for enrollment
- Admits only qualified students
- Charges reasonable tuition fees
- Offers up-to-date courses
- Maintains equipment for the training programs
- Employs instructors with program-related job experience
- Keeps classes to a reasonable size
- Provides guidance and job placement services

Remember, accreditation is your index of a school's commitment to its students and to offering them a high-quality education. And like colleges, accredited private career schools can offer federally backed financial aid programs that can help you pay for your training.

History of the School
A school doesn't have to be in business for twenty years to be good. But if it has been operating for a few years, then you have an indication that it is steady, established, and reliable.

Program Descriptions
Program descriptions can vary, depending on the training area. Generally, the more information given, the better. After reading this section, you should know what's involved in the training and how long it should take to complete the program.

Facilities and Equipment

The catalog will describe the school's facilities and equipment. It is a good idea to review this information before you visit the school. (When you visit the school, you should check out the facilities and equipment advertised in the catalog.)

Admissions Policy

Most catalogs say that your interest in the training program is the most important factor in being accepted into a program. This is true. But the catalog should review the school's admissions requirements. Do you need a high school diploma or General Educational Development (GED) test, which leads to a high school equivalency diploma? Many schools will give you a basic skills test just to make sure that you are able to handle the training.

Enrollment Dates

Many schools say they have an open door policy. This doesn't mean that you can start any time you want. However, most schools will offer several starting dates during the year to help you get started as soon as possible. These dates will often appear in the school catalog.

Tuition and Refund Policies

These policies are very important to understand before you decide to enroll. It is not unusual for the tuition costs to be listed on a sheet separate from the catalog. (Tuition information changes more quickly than the general information.) In addition, there should be a stated refund policy for students who find it necessary to leave school. The amount of the refund depends on how long a student has been in training. The refund policy will be different from school to school, but it should be clearly stated.

Financial Assistance

Several federal and state grants and loans are available to assist students attending private career schools. If the school does not list any, ask why.

Placement

Any good school includes job placement as part of its program, and the catalog should include this information. Career planning services should be part of the tuition costs. The school ought to have an active placement office, because that's the bottom line for both of you. However, keep in mind that no one can guarantee you a job, and no school should guarantee you a job.

Administrative Policies

A good catalog will mention the rules regarding attendance and conduct, grading, the dress code (if applicable), and the available counseling and tutoring services.

If the catalog covers all the categories of information listed here and the training program seems like the one you want, then you are ready for the next step in planning for your future—calling the school and making an appointment to talk to a school official.

Chapter 4

Deciding Factors

The school visit (the admissions interview and school tour) is one of the most important stages in your career search. This chapter outlines the questions you should ask yourself, the interviewer, and students currently attending the school. The answers you receive about the training, admissions policies, enrollment process, costs, placement activities, and school rules will help you to decide whether there is a good match between you and the school.

WHAT ARE PRIVATE CAREER SCHOOLS REALLY LIKE?

Private career schools are like people—each is unique. Yet, some generalizations can be made.

- Private career schools often specialize in several training areas.
- Most schools are located in the main business district of a city or town or in a nearby business area. Sometimes, these schools are in a building with other businesses.
- Carpeting, a receptionist, and a pleasant waiting area combine to make these schools look more like businesses than university and college campuses.

- These schools fit a lot into a little space, and some have additional classroom space in other buildings within a couple of miles of the main building.

- These schools are student oriented. Enrollment averages 300 students. Classes are small, with 15 to 25 students per class. When you first visit these schools, they will seem friendly and relaxed. But once you have made the commitment to your training, the school becomes as concerned with your success as you are.

- Programs may be as short as three months for some careers or as long as two years for other careers. (Some schools offer three- and four-year programs.) Programs attended full-time can take up to 35 hours per week. Several shifts may be available, offering classes in the morning, afternoon, and evening.

- Tuition costs depend on the length of training and the level of skills taught. Training can cost from $2,000 to $9,000 per year.

- The staff is small and made up of people you will see often. Usually, the school's staff includes a director, admissions personnel, financial aid counselors, student services personnel, a placement person, and several teachers.

- Private career schools are skills oriented and job oriented. Their main interest is in teaching the specific skills that are needed in today's marketplace.

- Improving your marketability and training you for a job are the most important concerns of any private career school. Schools continue to succeed because people like you leave as satisfied customers.

VISITING THE SCHOOL

The real test of any school will be how you feel about it. So, make a date to see the school. Although most schools are prepared to talk with walk-ins, an appointment will give you more time to discuss their programs and your future.

Make the appointment for a time when you know students are in class. This will give you a chance to see classes in action and to talk with students in the program of interest to you.

When you arrive at the school, you may be given a brief information sheet to fill out. This gives the admissions office some background on you so that the interview will be more helpful to you.

While at the school, you should ask yourself whether it is a place you want to be five days a week for six months to a year or more. Do *you* think you can handle the skills required? Do the people at the school seem as if they want to help you learn and plan for your future?

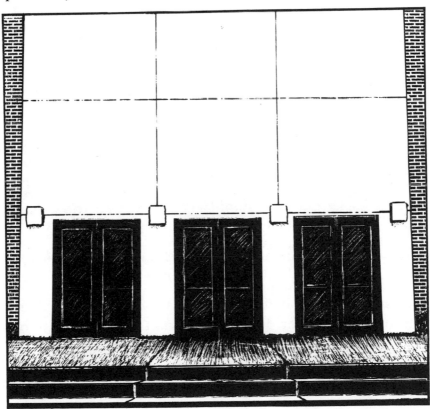

QUESTIONS AND ANSWERS

Your meeting with a member of the admissions staff is the time to ask questions. Be sure to ask about the training courses, admissions policies, enrollment process, costs, placement activities, and school rules. Your interview should also include a tour of the school.

The Training

You will want to know what the training involves.

- How long is the training? How many hours per day and days per week are required? What class schedules are offered?

- What are the skill objectives? What is learned in what amount of time?

- What kinds of things should you expect to do? How much of the course is hands-on as opposed to theory and lecture?

- How many courses are individualized, and how many courses involve working in a team? How many other students will be in the class?

- What kinds of facilities are used, and what kind of equipment is available? How much of the equipment is shared with other students?

- What background do the teachers have? For how many years and how long ago did they work in the field?

- Will your program include an actual work experience, training in a real business or industry?

- If you have a problem with part of the course, are there tutoring fees? If you don't pass a part of the course, can you repeat it without paying again?

- What kind of job can you expect to get once you finish the training?

- Are you required to take a certification test or licensing exam before you can get a job? Will you be able to apply for certification/licensing when the training is over?

- Once on a job, if more training is needed in an area, can you come back for refresher training?

Things to Think About

There are no right or wrong answers to these questions. The answers will vary depending on the specific training program. However, think very carefully about some of the answers.

Most career schools stress hands-on training, learning by doing. The point of this method is to train students as quickly as possible to be job ready.

Look carefully at the classroom teaching methods. Individualized instruction encourages the development of certain skills, but it also relies on the student to stick to the task. Group instruction is more structured, with the teacher setting the pace. You will need to think about what learning environment is best for you and whether the school's structure matches your learning style.

Note the student-teacher ratio. It is one of the most important factors in the classroom. Teachers can be more aware of your needs if they are not teaching too many students at one time.

Career schools are geared to helping students from different backgrounds. A good school knows that certain parts of the training may be difficult. Therefore, many schools offer tutoring as well as a chance to repeat part of the course, if needed.

Even if training is thorough, a particular job may use a lot of skills in one or two specialized areas. Many schools allow students to come back at night to review and refresh their training in an area. See if the school has a standing invitation to help you once you are on the job.

Admissions Policies

Admissions standards have been set because the school knows what it takes to succeed in specific careers. They want you to be able to reach your goal. You will want to ask:

- Is a high school diploma or GED required?

- Is there an admissions test? What happens if the scores are too low?

Thinks to Think About

The school should stress the importance of a high school diploma or GED because most employers do. Even with the completion of solid training, many employers use the diploma/GED to screen out prospective employees. The school may say that you can get in the program without a diploma, but, in most cases, schools prefer that students get a GED before the training is finished. In making this policy, the school is being honest with you, knowing that your chances are limited without this credential. But don't worry or be discouraged if you don't have a diploma or GED. The school will be very helpful in telling you how to reach this goal.

Private career schools often make each students take a test before any training begins. Tests are scary to a lot of people, but these tests will help the school judge your basic skills in reading and mathematics. Schools don't want you to enroll in a program that you can't handle. They are about success, not failure. If your scores fall below minimum, other choices will be provided. Some schools have a class to help you work on your skills, and others know where to send you to improve your scores.

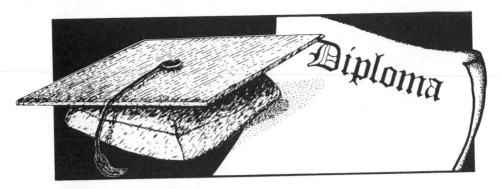

The Enrollment Process

You begin the enrollment process when you first meet with the school official. Schools handle enrollment in several different ways, but you will want to ask:

- When is the next enrollment date for a training class? How long does the enrollment process usually take?

- Is there an admissions test? If so, when may the test be taken, and when will the results be available?

- Is there a second formal interview? Does it involve one person or a committee?

- What information does the school need before enrollment can be completed?

- When will students know if they have been accepted?

Things to Think About

The enrollment process begins with your first interview. You will probably meet with the director of the school or with another school official. Remember, your training will be a great investment of your time, energy, and money. This is the time for you to get to know the school and for the school to get to know you.

The school official will be looking at your background, your test scores, and, most of all, your interest in the field you have chosen. A school's chances of having a satisfied customer depend on this information and believing that its staff is offering you good advice based on years of experience.

The Costs

The cost of training is not cheap and will vary depending on the training field and program length. The homework you have done will help you to do some comparison shopping. Although each school's tuition is different, schools should charge similar prices for similar training. If the costs of attending the school you are visiting are higher than those of other schools you have read about, ask why. Other questions you will want to ask are:

- What is included in the tuition?
- Is the registration fee included in the tuition, or is it a separate fee?
- Are books and supplies separate, and, if so, what are the estimated expenses?
- Are tools provided, or must the student pay an additional fee for some or all of the tools required for training?
- Are uniforms supplied, or do they cost extra?
- If additional help is needed, must the student pay a separate fee?
- When training is over, does the student keep the books, supplies, tools, uniforms, etc., or do they go back to the school?

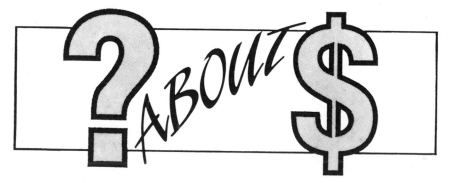

Things to Think About

At this point, you, as the buyer, should be looking for hidden costs. Paying for the training will become a big issue, so you must make sure that you know *all* of the training costs. (Many schools include textbooks as part of the tuition.) Remember, there will probably be an application fee, which will not be refunded if you are not accepted by the school.

Placement Activities

Getting a job is the bottom line. You will want to find out how much assistance the school provides and how successful it has been in placing graduates. Questions you will want to ask include:

- What has your placement rate been for the past year or two?

- What companies have hired your graduates? What positions did they get, and what was their starting wage? Do you have a current list of employers?

- How many school staff members are involved in placement, and how many students do they work with at a time?

- Does the placement office staff help find part-time jobs for students who are in training? What kind of help is provided? Do placement officers arrange interviews? Do they help prepare a finished resume for each student? Do they review job applications completed by the student?

- For how long will the school work with a student on job placement following graduation?

- Will the school continue to help the graduate if job placement assistance is needed later on?

Things to Think About

Schools do not guarantee jobs. However, a good school will put a lot of energy into assisting its students in getting jobs. The training program should include instruction in making up a resume, completing job applications, contacting employers, and handling interviews. If the job involves meeting the public, there should be instruction on proper dress and telephone manner. Practice interviews should be a part of the job placement program and, if possible, videotaping (to help you judge your interviewing skills) should be available.

Although training you to contact employers may be part of the instruction, the placement office should also have a list of employers with whom they have worked. Placement personnel should be able to refer you to these employers for job openings.

Some schools even offer placement assistance after you have found your first job. This means that the school will assist you in finding a job years later if you return for help. This may be important to you in the future, but right now the most important assurance is that the school can help you get that first job.

The School Rules

The rules should be listed in the catalog. The interview will give you a chance to understand them better. Private career schools are not like high school, and there won't be pages of rules. You are an adult and will be treated like an adult. You will need to review the rules and ask:

- Is there a dress code, and what does it mean?
- What are the attendance rules, and how are they upheld?

Things to Think About

In many schools, you will be expected to wear the same gear worn on the job. Requiring proper dress and behavior and steady attendance is a form of on-the-job training.

Most schools have strong attendance rules for the simple reason that if you aren't there, you can't learn and won't earn. If you miss too many days, you may have to meet with the director. If you miss classes too often, you may have to repeat part of the course and may even be asked to leave the school.

The school's attendance policies train you to become a good employee with good work habits. At the time you sign the enrollment agreement, you are making your first strong commitment to be there each day to learn new skills.

WALKING THROUGH THE SCHOOL

Following the interview, the admissions officer should offer you a tour. Although there will be a lot of things to see at one time, you should just try to get a strong feeling for the way the school serves students. Ask if you can sit in on one of the classes for a few minutes. While in the classroom, ask yourself the following questions:

- Is the textbook material easy to read?

- Is the teacher lecturing, or leading the class in hands-on instruction?

- Do students seem to have enough to do, and are they enjoying what they are doing?

- Does there seem to be enough equipment for each student, or does it look as though students have to take turns?

- Does the area look clean?

The school probably will have a student lounge. Ask if you may spend a few minutes in the lounge to talk with other students. You might ask the following questions:

- Are you getting the training you expected?
- Do you think you're getting your money's worth?
- Do you know other students who graduated, and did they get good jobs?

As you walk through the halls, notice the displays on the walls. They can tell you a lot about the school. If you don't see anything, you should be cautious. Some typical items are:

- School membership plaques and licenses
- A part-time jobs board
- A display of recent graduates and the jobs they got
- A display of student projects
- Awards given to outstanding students in the school
- News about upcoming student events, meetings, and graduations

PAYING FOR THE TRAINING

As you have already read, training can be costly. The three main forms of financial aid available to assist students who need help are:

- Federal scholarships or grants that do not have to be repaid
- Federally insured loans that must be repaid (although payments and interest charges may not begin until after you complete the program)
- Part-time employment

In addition, many states offer programs of grants and scholarships.

In order to find out how much financial aid you need, you first must know the cost of a training program. The next step is to find out how much you will need to pay. To find this out, you have to fill out a Financial Aid Form or Family Financial Statement. Both forms ask you to answer questions about your family's total income and savings and your own expenses for clothing, food, health care, and housing. You may also indicate any other unusual expenses. The difference between the cost of the training and the amount you are expected to pay is called your financial need and is the basis upon which financial aid is allowed.

The financial aid forms can be very confusing. This is another area in which the private career school can help you. Each school has a financial aid staff person to work with you. He or she is ready to go through the forms with you and tell you what information you must provide. Keep calm: it may take several weeks for the federal government to determine if you qualify for financial aid.

Don't forget that there are *deadlines* for requesting financial aid. Find out when the financial aid application is due. Even if the deadline is approaching and you are not sure whether you want to attend a school, you can still send in your financial aid application. Your financial aid can be used at any eligible school. But remember, the amount of aid may change because the determined need is based on the difference between the cost of the training and your available resources.

Please note these two bits of advice on financial aid. First, the government is very serious these days about the repayment of government loans for education. Second, be sure you are clear about which part of your aid is actually a loan. Find out when you must begin to pay the loan back.

In addition, you may want to look for a part-time job. Many schools have a part-time jobs board. The jobs listed will not be glamorous or pay well, but they can provide a way to get the money you need while in training.

SPEAKING UP

The following checklist will help you remember the things you want to ask at the school. Even if you are not a person who usually asks a lot of questions, you must remember that what you learn in your school visit will affect your future. Your concerns and questions are one way you can let the school staff know that you are serious about your future career.

Seeing the school will give you a lot to think about. Once you have seen what the school looks like, how it runs, what's involved in the training, and how much it will cost, you can begin to make a decision.

CHECKLIST FOR THE SCHOOL VISIT

The Training

How long does it take to complete training?

What are the choices for attending class? Are classes offered during the day and night?

What skills will be taught?

How much of the training is hands-on, and how much is lecture?

How many students are in a class?

What equipment is used?

Is there an opportunity to get work experience?

Is tutoring available?

Can a student repeat a part of the course if needed?

What kind of job can be obtained when the training is over?

Is a certification test or licensing exam required before getting a job in the field?

Can a student return later for refresher training?

Admissions Policies

Is a high school diploma or GED required?

Is there an admissions test, and how are the scores used?

The Enrollment Process

When is the next enrollment date for a training class?

If there is an admissions test, when may the test be taken?

Is there another interview before acceptance?

What information does the school need before acceptance?

The Costs

What is included in the tuition?

Is the registration fee separate?

What are the estimated expenses for books and materials?

Are tools provided, or must they be paid for separately?

Are uniforms supplied?

If extra help is needed, is there an additional fee?

Placement Activities

What has been the school's placement rate for the last year or two?

What companies have hired graduates?

What is the typical beginning position, and what is the starting salary?

How many students does the placement staff work with at a time?

What does the placement office do to assist in locating part-time jobs for students while they are in training?

What does the placement staff do to help in getting jobs for the graduate?

Are skills to make the graduate more employable part of the training, and when does this instruction begin?

The School Rules

What are the school's rules for behavior and dress?

What are the attendance rules, and how are they upheld?

Chapter 5

Going for It

In this chapter, you will review the fact-finding missions you have completed so far. You have researched your career options and are ready to enroll in a training program. Are you worried about making a decision, signing the contract? This chapter reviews the parts of the school contract and answers the question, "What does signing the contract mean to me?"

COMPLETED MISSIONS

The visit to the school is completed. This means you have come a long way in planning your future.

Look at the fact-finding missions you have completed so far:

- You thought about the difference a good job can make in building the way of life you want. A good job can make a difference in the amount of money you can earn in the next year or two, and it can make a difference in your earning power over a working lifetime. It can make a difference in how important you are to a company. It can give you the opportunity to continue to learn new things, to get better jobs, and to grow. It can enable you to do interesting work that has a future. A good job can make a difference in how you think about yourself. It can make you feel valued and increase your feeling of self-respect.

- You took some time to look at yourself—to think about what is important to you, what interests you, and what your abilities are.

- You talked to people about their jobs. You talked to counselors and librarians to get information about certain occupations. You did your homework and know what is required for the career. You know about the working conditions, the pay, and the promotion opportunities. You considered whether this career will be around in the future.

- You made a decision to find out how you can be trained for the career you have picked.

- You located the schools and contacted them to get information on training programs.

- You learned what you can expect a school to provide.

- You looked at school catalogs and considered, among other things, whether these schools seem stable.

- You visited the chosen school and asked questions about it and the programs it offers.

- During the interview and the tour, you listened to the school official, paid careful attention to the classes in session, inspected the facilities and the equipment, observed the instructors, and talked with the students.

- You have found out whether the school is able to deliver the training it promises.

- You checked on financial aid, and you know what it will take to pay for the training.

The school has done everything it can to interest you in the training, and you have thoroughly reviewed the school and the program of interest.

So now what?

Now it is time to make another important decision: the decision to sign the contract and enroll in the training program. You have finished the research part of planning for your future, and you know the factors you should consider in selecting a private career school.

Now is the time for action!

You may talk to your parents, your friends, and your spouse. You may talk to a counselor. But now comes the hardest part—taking a deep breath and saying yes. When you do, you will be agreeing to take the time to change your life, to make a difference in where you will be in five years.

THE BUSINESS AT HAND

If you answered yes, then it's back to business for a moment, and the enrollment agreement is definitely business. The agreement is a legal contract. The school is the seller, and you are the buyer. You will be legally responsible for the financial arrangements agreed to in the contract.

Reading the contract carefully is a way to run a final check on the school. First of all, be sure you *read every line of the contract*. Each school's contract will be different, but every good school will have the terms of the agreement clearly spelled out.

Contracts always seem hard to read, and parts of them are in small print. If reading something while someone else is waiting for you to finish makes you uncomfortable (and it does for most people), then say that you would like a few minutes to yourself to go over the contract. Although a school official may go through the contract with you line by line, it's perfectly OK to ask for some private time to consider what you are signing.

The following items should be included somewhere in the contract:

- The school will be listed as the seller, and your name will be typed in as the buyer. There should be a space in which is typed the exact name of the training program. A space or spaces with the length of the training in terms of a period of time and/or clock hours should appear. The beginning and ending dates for the training should also be included.

- There will be an item-by-item listing of the costs. Costs can include the registration fee, tuition, supplies, and books.

- There should be a section on the payment agreement. This section should state how a monthly payment plan works, when payments are due, whether there is a finance charge or interest due, and if prepayment is possible without penalty.

- There should be a stated policy about late payments, indicating whether there are late charges and/or other consequences (such as not being able to attend classes until the payment is made).

- It should be stated clearly whether there are additional costs if you need to extend your training beyond the designated dates.

- There should be a big section on the refund policy. These policies vary from school to school. However, you should make sure that the school's policies about the following situations are clearly stated:

  — You should know what percentage of any money that you have already paid will be returned to you if the school rejects you for training.

— You should know what the refund policy is if you cancel the contract *within* three days. (To officially cancel the contract, you will have to follow the school's procedures.)

— You should know what the policy is if you cancel *after* three days but before classes begin. (You should get a refund with a certain amount withheld.)

— Be sure to ask about partial-refund policies. Partial refunds that are linked to the length of time you have been in training should be possible. The length of training time and any refund amount should be spelled out in your contract.

— You should know from the contract how to officially withdraw from school, how to request a refund, and when you can expect to receive the refund.

• There should be a section explaining the school's standards for students in training and what situations might lead to dismissal. This information covers your attendance, behavior, and required grades.

• What you will receive at the completion of training (e.g., a certificate or diploma) should be indicated.

• A section covering the placement assistance available at no additional fee should be included. Remember, no reputable school will guarantee placement at the end of training. Be sure all the blanks have been filled in or have "XXX" in the space before you sign the contract.

The school official knows how hard it is to understand all the legal terms that must be in a contract, and he or she should explain any part you don't understand. The last thing the school wants is for you to feel nervous about signing the contract. It is not unusual for the school official to give you his or her phone number and tell you to call if you have any doubts or concerns. Although this is a serious matter because you are financially responsible to the school under the terms of the contract, it should also be a joyous day. The contract is a symbol of the commitment you have made to change the way you work and live. You will no longer just wonder what will happen in the future. You will have a course of action that can put you in control of your own tomorrow.

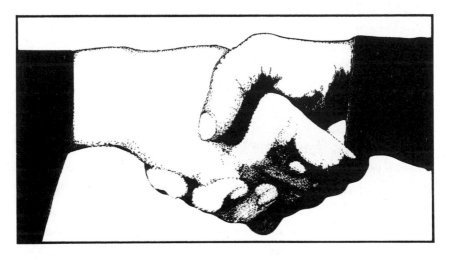

YOU WILL NOT BE ALONE

The goal of this guide has been accomplished if you have read through it, followed its suggestions, and started on the path to reaching your personal career goals.

But this guide would not be complete if it didn't include the greatest reason for choosing a private career school. Quite simply, this reason is that private career schools are made of people *who care about you.*

The people at career schools know that many individuals spent their years in public school just going along, not seeing the school as a place to succeed.

The career school staff knows that some people are in jobs that are going nowhere, aren't interesting, and don't make them feel good about themselves. Staff members understand that having a good job is important to many people, but that people often need to become more marketable before they can get a good job. The staff believes that education and training are the keys to getting careers that enable people to use their abilities to the fullest and to respect what they do to make a living.

In addition, the staff understands that sometimes life gets in the way—problems arise that need to be solved while students are in training.

Even before you enroll, you will see the private career school philosophy at work.

- The school looks more like a place of business than a high school or college campus.

- You're treated like a client or the buyer of an important service.

- You have several options for classes—schedules for days, afternoons, and evenings.

- You are tested for basic skills and know about the programs to improve your abilities.

- You aren't just given financial aid forms, you get help to complete them.

- You get assistance locating part-time jobs and may even get help finding a place to live while attending the school.

- There are bulletin boards with pictures of recent graduates, displays of student projects, and awards for students' achievements.

- The school accommodates all age groups—young and old—and people with different educational and work experience backgrounds.

Once you are in school, you will see further signs of these beliefs put into practice.

- Classes are small, allowing for more student-instructor time together.

- If you need more time on a subject, you can take it again.

- If you are absent from class for a day, someone will call to find out whether there is a problem.

- Staff members work with you on any problem that could keep you out of training.

- Monthly program awards recognize students' achievements as they move through the program.

- The school is involved in improving your marketability, which means working on your job-getting skills and on your personal appearance as well as on your career skills.

- A strong job placement office works with you to help get you on the job.

- You can call back and get advice and help once you are on the job.

You are the most important concern of the private career school. This is one of the few times in your life when there will be a whole group of people as involved in your success as you are.

This guide was written to help you take the steps to change your life. You now know how to go about making a sound decision to get the skills you need to achieve your goal or, rather, your *next* goal. As you grow older, you may want to strive to reach other goals, and now you know how to deal with any career possibility.

Good luck!

Job Profiles

The following is an alphabetized list of 107 job descriptions. All occupations listed may be prepared for by training at private career schools throughout the nation. Descriptions contain a definition of the job, a brief summary of job responsibilities, and information concerning the employment possibilities associated with that particular career.

Actor

To act out roles and a range of moods, actors use their natural abilities and skills learned during training. Actors often work long hours and must be able to remember scripts. They work mostly in theater, film, TV, and radio.

Air-Conditioning Technician

Putting in and fixing cooling equipment are the main duties of air-conditioning technicians. Many work for contractors and dealers. Others are self-employed.

Animal Trainer

Animal trainers prepare animals for a variety of purposes,

(continued)

including working in the show business and security industries and working with the handicapped. They evaluate the nature and ability of animals and set up programs to develop desired behavior. Trainers are identified according to the specific animal trained.

Appliance Repairer

Appliance repairers know how appliances work. They know where to look for problems and how to fix them. Most repairers work for small appliance stores and repair shops.

Architectural Engineering Technician

Architectural engineering technicians work closely with architects. They are involved in drafting designs; gathering data on materials, costs, equipment, and building times; writing descriptions for each job; building models; and helping prepare contracts. Most work for architecture and construction firms.

Artist, Commercial

Commercial artists design artwork for TV, product packages, greeting cards, and newspapers and magazines. Many specialize in advertising art. They work for corporations and advertising companies or are self-employed.

Artist, Fine

Fine artists usually sculpt or paint. They may sell their creations to galleries. Fine artists also work in the art departments of schools and colleges and in art museums.

Some become art critics for newspapers and magazines.

Auto Body Repairer

Auto body repairers restore car frames, removing dents and replacing damaged parts. They use special machines to repair cars. Most work in shops specializing in automotive repair. Others work for firms that maintain their own motor vehicles.

Automotive Technician

Automotive technicians are able to work on every phase of a car's operation. These technicians understand the electrical, mechanical, and electronic parts of each car. However, since the modern-day car has over 30,000 parts and is very complicated to work on, many choose to specialize in one area, such as bodywork, transmissions, tune-ups, and brakes. They need to know how to use diagnostic equipment. Automotive technicians work for auto dealers, repair shops, and taxi and auto-leasing companies.

Aviation Maintenance Technician

Aviation maintenance technicians (or airplane mechanics) maintain and inspect planes. They take engines apart, measure parts for wear, check for invisible cracks, and replace worn parts. They inspect planes for damage and stress. Most airplane mechanics work for airlines and aviation manufacturers or in general aviation.

Bank Teller

Bank tellers cash checks, deposit money, and withdraw

(continued)

funds for bank customers. Tellers begin their day before the bank opens and work after the bank is closed. For them, the workday begins with the receiving of and counting of cash. This cash is used for payments during the day, and the teller is responsible for its handling. Bank tellers also sort checks and deposit slips.

Barber

(see Hairstylist)

Bartender

Bartenders mix and serve alcoholic and nonalcoholic drinks to customers at bars. They follow standard recipes and mix ingredients, such as liquor, soda, water, and bitters, to prepare cocktails and other drinks. In addition to collecting money for drinks, bartenders order liquor and other supplies.

Blueprint Reader

Blueprint readers read the details of architectural and mechanical blueprints. They also estimate production costs to bid on jobs.

Boat Builder.

Boat builders construct, repair, and modify wooden boats, life rafts, and pontoons. They use blueprints and tools such as hand tools, power tools, scales, protractors, and measuring instruments.

Brickmason

Brickmasons build walls, fireplaces, barbecues, and chimneys. They use brick and mortar and may also have to work with other materials, such as cinder block. They must be able to handle heavy loads and be good at using plumb lines and levels. Most brickmasons work for building contractors. About one in seven is self-employed.

Broadcaster

Employed by TV and radio stations, broadcasters introduce programs, guests, and music and deliver news and live commercials. In small stations, they may operate the control board, sell advertising, and write news segments and commercials. Most work for radio stations, and the rest work for TV stations. (Nationwide, there are more than 700 TV stations and about 7,000 radio stations.)

Broadcasting Technician

Broadcasting technicians are responsible for getting a program on the air. They operate and maintain the electronic equipment used to transmit radio and TV programs. They also control the quality of the sound and/or picture being broadcast. They operate controls that switch shows from one camera or studio to another, from recorded to live programming, and from network to local programs.

Building Maintenance Technician

Building maintenance technicians keep buildings clean and in good working condition. Managing the upkeep of a building requires knowledge of heating systems, cleaning equipment, chemical cleaners, basic electricity, and plumbing repair. Most technicians are employed by building maintenance contractors and management firms.

Cabinetmaker

Cabinetmakers cut, shape, and assemble prepared wooden parts. They set up and operate woodworking machines and use hand tools to create and repair cabinets and furniture.

Carpenter

Carpenters must have the ability to solve mathematical and geometrical problems quickly. Their work is divided into two types: rough and finish carpentry. Rough carpentry includes erecting frames, rafters, and temporary structures. Finish work is done where appearance counts, such as in stairs, paneling, and floors.

Civil Engineering Technician

Civil engineering technicians assist civil engineers in planning, designing, and constructing highways, bridges, dams, harbors, airports, and pipelines, among other structures. They often specialize in a particular area of civil engineering. They figure costs and prepare materials. Sometimes, they survey, draft, and design.

Computer-Aided Drafter

Computer-aided drafters learn to generate computer design drawings and instructions required by manufacturers to produce a product. They often use a computer-aided design system.

Computer Programmer

Computer programmers convert statements of business problems, which are usually represented by detailed charts and graphs, into code that the computer reads. In addition, they correct program errors, prepare written instructions to help operating personnel during production runs, and analyze, review, and rewrite programs to increase productivity or to conform to new requirements.

Computer Service Technician

Installing and keeping systems working is the job of computer service technicians. Determining what is not working in the system is often the most difficult part of the job. These technicians use several types of testing equipment to locate the problem. They are employed by equipment manufacturers, maintenance service firms, and companies with large computers.

Construction Technologist

Construction technologists must know building codes and engineering requirements and be able to monitor craftworkers and subcontractors. They must be able to assist managers in inspecting, costing, and troubleshooting. These workers must have good judgment and good people skills.

Cosmetologist

Cosmetologists shampoo, cut, and style hair; give manicures; give facial treatments; and provide makeup for women. They may also straighten hair, give permanents, and lighten or darken hair color. Cosmetologists work in unisex hairstyling shops, salons, department stores, hospitals, and hotels. About one third own their own businesses.

Court Reporter

(see Shorthand Reporter)

Culinary Arts Specialist

Culinary arts specialists work with cooks and other kitchen workers who prepare foods for restaurants. They select and develop recipes and manage the preparation, cooking, and serving of meats, sauces, vegetables, soups, and other foods.

Data Entry Specialist

Data entry specialists handle transcription and typing duties. They produce letters and reports on computers and other high-speed machines that store material in memory. Operators use commands to enter, store, retrieve, and delete information. These specialists work for service organizations, such as educational institutions and hospitals; for government agencies; and for temporary-employment agencies.

Data Processor

Data processors enter information into computer systems, feed instructions to and operate the computer, develop plans the computer follows to produce information, and decide the data processing techniques used to solve a problem. Specialties within data processing include keypunching, computer operations, programming, and systems analysis.

Dealer

Dealers must understand dice, roulette, and card concepts. They trade paper money for playing chips and for coin money. In addition to announcing winning numbers, dealers must figure payable odds for winning bets. They also pay winning bets and collect losing bets. Dealers conduct gambling tables in gambling establishments.

Dental Assistant

Dental assistants prepare patients for treatment, pass instruments and materials to the dentist, prepare fillings, and develop X rays. Some also maintain patient records, make appointments, and handle billing and payments. Most dental assistants work in dental offices for individual dentists or for group practices. Others work in public health departments and clinics.

Dental Laboratory Technician

Using their knowledge of dental anatomy and working from a dentist's prescription, dental laboratory technicians make false teeth, create metal and porcelain crowns and inlays, construct bridges, and make braces. These technicians use small hand-held instruments. Most work in commercial laboratories. Many own their own labs.

Dental Receptionist

(see Medical/Dental Receptionist)

Diamond Cutter

Diamond cutters rate a diamond and determine its grain structure. They decide how a diamond should be cut. Diamond cutters also repair broken diamonds and modernize old-style cuts. In addition, they are knowledgeable in the areas of purchasing and selling diamonds. Some specialize in diamond buying and grading.

Diesel Mechanic

Diesel mechanics care for and repair diesel engines. They

(continued)

must know how to run tests on the engine, make adjustments, and repair parts. Most work for trucking companies, bus lines, construction firms, highway departments, and manufacturers.

Dietetics Technician

Dietetics technicians are trained to assist a dietitian in planning meals. These workers also supervise the preparation and serving of food. They are responsible for food purchases and accounts. Technicians who work in hospitals and nursing centers may also be responsible for monitoring dietary plans developed by a dietitian, explaining these plans to patients, and making follow-up visits to patients' homes.

Diver

Divers build, save, inspect, and demolish underwater structures. Their services are needed by a variety of employers. Their work requires excellent physical health and may involve considerable travel.

Drafter

Drafters make drawings that show the exact dimensions of an object from various sides. They work from rough sketches made by scientists, designers, engineers, and architects. Drafters also figure the strength, quality, quantity, and costs of materials. These workers usually specialize in an area. Specialties include electronic, electrical, mechanical, structural, architectural, and aeronautical drafting. (See also Computer-aided Drafter.)

Dressmaker

Dressmakers usually use a pattern to cut and sew material

to a customer's exact size. Some dressmakers also design garments. Some specialize in complete handmade garments, and others make alterations only. Dressmaking requires the ability to do neat, careful work. Most dressmakers work in shops, clothing stores, and department stores. Some are self-employed.

Electrician

There are two types of electricians: construction and maintenance electricians. Construction electricians work on buildings and, following outlines and regulations, install the wiring that operates heating and air-conditioning, lighting, power, and refrigerating equipment. Maintenance electricians keep electrical equipment in working order in plants, offices, and homes. They may work from blueprints and diagrams to find problems and use meters and other devices to test equipment.

Electrologist

Electrologists use electricity to permanently remove unwanted hair from the body for cosmetic reasons. They prepare customers for treatment, decide the correct needle size for the epilator (electrical instrument that removes hair), and handle posttreatment activities. Electrologists are self-employed or employed in beauty salons.

Electronics Specialist

Electronics specialists are involved in the development and testing, manufacturing, and servicing of electronic equipment and systems. Because the field is so technical, those in electronics specialize in any one of several branches, such as TV and radio, sonar, digital, communications, industrial, biomedical, navigations, aeronautical, and computer electronics.

Emergency Medical Technician

Emergency medical technicians travel to the location of an emergency, evaluate a patient's condition, and determine the immediate medical care needed. Lifesaving measures are taken, such as maintaining an open airway, restoring heartbeat, checking bleeding, treating for shock, and fixing bones, until the time the patient is delivered to the hospital. Most EMTs are employed by city emergency units, police and fire departments, private ambulance companies, and hospitals.

Engraver

Jewelry, mugs, trophies, trays, and other personal objects are beautified and made more personal by engravers. They carve designs and engrave words and sentences as specified by customers. Engravers usually work with precious metals and must have a steady hand. They are employed by retail jewelry shops and department stores.

Fashion Designer

Fashion designers are creative artists who can produce clothes to serve the public's needs and desires. These designers create original styles by drawing sketches. They also work with colors and fabrics. Designers may specialize in high-fashion clothing, leisure wear, furs, sleepwear, men's clothing, and children's clothing.

Fashion Illustrator

Fashion illustrators bring fashions to life through their drawings of clothes and accessories. Their work appears in magazines, newspapers, and mail advertisements. For the most part, these illustrators work in the advertising department of large retail stores and in ad agencies.

Fashion Merchandiser

Fashion merchandisers select and resell clothing lines to the public. Depending on the size of the store, the job of fashion merchandising may be the responsibility of one person or of many. In larger stores, it may be handled by specialists—buyers, managers, fashion coordinators, display artists, and fashion promoters, among others—who all work together. Fashion merchandisers also review inventory and set pricing guidelines. Most work for department stores and small shops.

Flower Arranger

Flower arrangers use fresh-cut, dried, and artificial flowers to create wreaths, bouquets, and other attractive floral arrangements for special occasions and for display in homes and offices. Most flower arrangers work in flower shops and in department stores. Some are self-employed.

Food Service Specialist

Catering firms, restaurants, hospitals, hotels, and airlines employ food service specialists. These professionals handle menu planning, the purchase of food supplies, food cost control, health conditions, and customer relations. It is their job to see that food is properly and attractively prepared and that the necessary equipment is in good working order. They are also in charge of inventory control and monitoring employees.

Gemologist

Gemologists judge the quality and evaluate the market value of precious stones. They are chiefly employed by importers, wholesalers, and retailers of gemstones.

Gunsmith

Guns need the regular repair and maintenance provided by skilled gunsmiths. Gunsmiths make new parts for guns when necessary. Often, they are self-employed, working out of hobby shops. Some gunsmiths work in sporting goods stores or in the sporting goods department of larger stores. Others are employed by the manufacturers of small weapons.

Hairstylist (Barber and Hairdresser)

Hairstylists cut, style, and color hair. They must be licensed by the state in which they work. In preparation for the licensing exam, hairstylists are trained for a specified number of hours. Many work in small, independent shops and unisex salons. More than half are self-employed.

Heating Mechanic

Heating mechanics install oil, gas, and electrical heating units; supply lines; ducts; and pumps. They connect wiring and controls and check units for proper operation. Most are employed by cooling and heating contractors and dealers, fuel oil dealers, and utility companies. Some are self-employed.

Heavy-Equipment Operator

Heavy-equipment operators move tons of dirt and construction materials and erect steel beams and girders. They need to judge distances and heights and must control a variety of levers, pedals, and buttons. They usually operate bulldozers, cranes, trench diggers, and paving machines, among other types of heavy construction equipment. Most heavy-equipment operators work for contractors building dams, highways, airports, factories, offices, and apartment buildings.

Horsemanship Specialist

Riders, trainers, and riding instructors are all horsemanship specialists. These specialists must know about horse care, horse anatomy and illnesses, the different types of horses, the care of stables, and the types of horse-related equipment. These professionals work in small and large horse operations, in community recreational departments that have stables, and in camps.

Horticulturist

Horticulturists grow orchard and garden plants, using their knowledge of plants, ideal growing conditions, and plant bugs and diseases. Some work in greenhouses, where commercial growing is usually done and where business and management procedures must be applied. Horticulturists also work in garden centers and flower shops. Many are self-employed.

Hotel-Motel Manager

Hotel-motel managers control reservations and sales, housekeeping, and food and beverage operations. A specially trained management staff, headed by a general manager and several assistant managers, ensures that the business is run profitably. These managers work in small hotels and large hotel and motel chains. About a third are self-employed.

Illustrator

Illustrators must spend hours over drawing boards to produce neat finished work. They contribute black-and-white and color illustrations and diagrams to books, magazines, pamphlets, maps, newspapers, and technical and medical

(continued)

publications. Depending on the employer's needs, illustrators sketch or create imaginative artwork to represent written concepts and ideas. (See also Fashion Illustrator.)

Instrumentation Specialist

Instrumentation specialists make sure that hydraulic, electrical, electronic, and mechanical equipment is performing properly. They may also be involved in the development, design, service, and repair of complex measuring and control devices. They are employed by the industries that need this special equipment in order to function.

Interior Designer

Making rooms and areas more attractive and functional is the job of interior designers. These professionals plan the layout, color schemes, and furnishings of an area. They also buy the furnishings and manage craftworkers. Most work for interior design companies and department stores.

Jewelry Designer

Jewelry designers work with gemstones, gold, silver, lucite, and other materials. These designers create bracelets, rings, necklaces, and other objects for personal adornment. They make original designs either for an individual customer or for a line of costume jewelry for mass production.

Legal Assistant/Paralegal

Legal assistants and paralegals assist lawyers in case research, real estate transactions, document preparation, compiling customer history, and investigations. Short of making legal decisions, practicing in a court of law, and advising clients, a paralegal may handle many tasks formerly handled only by lawyers.

Legal Secretary

Legal secretaries trained in the law and in legal procedures are needed by attorneys and law offices. They must have knowledge of legal terms. Legal secretaries undertake research and prepare and type briefs and other legal documents.

Locksmith

Locksmiths install locks, fix damaged locks, pick locks, and make duplicate keys. An important part of a locksmith's job is recommending security measures to customers. Some locksmiths put in burglar alarms and security systems. Locksmiths are employed in small shops. Many are self-employed.

Loss Prevention Officer

(see Security Officer)

Machinist

Machinists work from blueprints to determine the machines to be used in production. They choose from a variety of milling machines, lathes, planes, grinders, drill presses, boring machines, and other equipment. They set

(continued)

up machines, adjust equipment (sometimes within a millionth of an inch), and repair parts. Machinists are employed in the metalworking industries, including the automobile, electrical equipment, and transportation equipment industries.

Makeup Artist

Makeup artists use rubber, plastic, wax, paint, and powder to create a variety of special effects for film, TV, and theater productions. They also use cosmetics to enhance the appearance of actors on film, on stage, in TV commercials, and in print advertisements. Some work as beauty advisers in salons. Others work for cosmetics companies, helping them to promote their products.

Marine Technician

Marine technicians perform various tasks on board ship. They must be familiar with the wide variety of advanced and alternative methods used to maintain, operate, and navigate small sailing vessels and power vessels. Marine technicians may inspect, adjust, repair, and maintain sails and rigging.

Massage Therapist

Massage therapists aid people in restoring and maintaining good health. Massage therapy may be used in programs of physical therapy, rehabilitative therapy, occupational therapy, physical fitness, nutrition, geriatrics, chiropractic, and holistic health. Whether for cure, rehabilitation, or general health maintenance, the job of the massage therapist requires good people skills.

Mechanical Engineering Technician

Mechanical engineering technicians work out accurate

dimensions, manufacturing procedures, production schedules, and costs. In addition, they assist in designing. Mechanical engineering technicians often specialize in such areas as aeronautical, automobile, industrial, electrical, and electronic engineering.

Medical Assistant

Medical assistants help with the preparation and treatment of a patient. They may take and record the patient's weight, temperature, pulse, and blood pressure. In addition, assistants aid the physician in minor surgical procedures and other treatments. They may also perform laboratory tests. In small offices, they are responsible for maintaining patient records, scheduling appointments, filing insurance forms, ordering supplies, and performing other office management duties.

Medical/Dental Receptionist

Medical/dental receptionists are responsible for making appointments for patients. They may also be required to schedule tests, answer the phone and screen calls, maintain patient records, type letters, and handle all billing and bookkeeping duties.

Medical Laboratory Technician

Medical laboratory technicians perform tests according to standardized lab practices. They collect and examine samples of tissue, blood, and other fluids and prepare and stain slides for detection of microorganisms and analysis of chemical components. Some technicians specialize in microbiology, hematology, and parasitology, among other areas. Most work in hospitals, clinics, and laboratories.

Medical Office Manager

Medical office managers run the day-to-day operation of medical offices. These managers hire and supervise other employees, order medical and office supplies, bill patients, maintain records, fill out insurance forms, and keep the books. Most medical office managers are employed in larger physicians' offices and by group practices.

Medical Secretary

Medical secretaries combine their knowledge of secretarial skills with their knowledge of medical terms and hospital, clinic, and laboratory procedures. They must use office equipment to maintain medical charts, reports, and correspondence. (They take dictation in shorthand or use transcribing machines.) Their responsibilities may include preparing and sending bills to patients and recording appointments.

Motion Pictures/Television Production Specialist

Motion pictures/television production specialists include producers, directors, camera operators, editors, and technical staff members. These specialists work together to produce movies, TV commercials, corporate films, training films, education films, and other types of motion pictures. Those working in motion pictures must know about film and cameras, lighting, special effects, visuals, sound, and other film techniques and specifications.

Motorcycle Mechanic

Motorcycle mechanics work on motorcycles, minibikes, snowmobiles, outboard motors, mopeds, and other vehicles and equipment powered by small gasoline engines. Like automobiles, motorcycles and these other machines need servicing and repair. Their spark plugs, ignition points, brakes, valves, and other electrical and mechanical parts need regular maintenance. Most motorcycle mechanics work for motorcycle dealers. Some maintain police motorcycles for city governments.

Musical Instrument Maker

Musical instrument makers design, construct, decorate, and repair musical instruments, including such popular handcrafted instruments as guitars and mandolins. They need to have a fine understanding of the principles of sound (acoustics) in order to create and repair instruments capable of high-quality sound. Nowadays, instrument makers must know how to apply electrical and electronic technology to some instruments.

Nurse, Vocational

Licensed vocational nurses assist in the treatment and care of patients. They provide bedside nursing care, such as taking temperatures and blood pressures, changing dressings, providing medicines, and assisting physicians and registered nurses in examining patients. Specializations include intensive care unit, burn unit, and delivery and recovery room nursing. Most work in hospitals. Others are employed in nursing homes, clinics, and other long-term health-care facilities.

Nurse's Aide

Nurse's aides are responsible for making patients comfortable and providing basic care in hospitals, nursing homes, and other medical facilities. (Men who work in this field are called orderlies.) These workers answer pa-

(continued)

tients' bell calls, serve meals, and feed, bathe, and dress patients. They assist patients in getting out of bed and walking. They also change beds. Nurse's aides may be responsible for taking temperatures, giving massages, and setting up medical equipment. Some work as ward clerks. Nurse's aides work under the supervision of registered nurses and licensed practical nurses.

Office Machine Repairer

Office machine repairers fix typewriters, calculators, dictating machines, postage meters, and copying equipment. They replace parts and clean, oil, and adjust machines. These repairers must be able to fix problems on the spot or move machines to the shop. Most office machine repairers work for manufacturing companies and dealers.

Operating Room Technician

Operating room technicians specialize in operating room procedures and equipment. They help set up the room with the instruments, equipment, sterile linens, and fluids needed for an operation. These professionals prepare the patient for an operation, washing, shaving, and sterilizing the operative area of the patient. They also position the patient on the operating table. During surgery, they pass instruments and other supplies to the surgeon. Operating room technicians may assist in administering transfusions and other injections. They also operate lights, suction machines, and other equipment.

Optometric Assistant

Optometric assistants specialize in providing support services for optometrists. (Optometrists are doctors who specialize in correcting vision through prescribed lenses or eye exercises.) These assistants take patients' case histories, record the results of eye exams, keep patient records, schedule appointments, and handle bookkeeping and filing. In a shop, they may fit customers with glasses and repair frames. Most optometric assistants work in optometrists' offices. Others work for health clinics.

Orderly

(see Nurse's Aide)

Painter

Painters apply paint, varnish, and other finishes to decorate and protect interior and exterior building surfaces. Painters sand or scrape away old paint, fill nail holes, remove grease, and repaint the surfaces of wood, plaster, concrete, metal, masonry, and drywall. They must be able to mix paints and match colors. Many painters work for contractors engaged in new construction and remodeling. Large-property managers also hire painters. About one fourth of all painters are self-employed.

Paperhanger

Paperhangers decorate with wallpaper, fabric, and vinyl to enhance wall surfaces. They must measure, size, align, and smooth all wall covering to hang materials professionally. Paperhangers work for painting and decorator contractors, or they own their own businesses.

Paralegal

(see Legal Assistant/Paralegal)

Pet Groomer

Pet groomers clean and groom pets. Some provide boarding facilities for pets and care for animals over an extended period of time. Pet shops, pet departments of large stores, and kennels require the services of professionals who have been trained to properly feed, exercise, and maintain pets. Those in pet grooming and kennel management are also employed by humane societies and are self-employed.

Photographer

Photographers usually specialize in a particular area. Commercial photographers take pictures for catalogs, cookbooks, and magazines and newspaper ads. Industrial photographers take pictures of corporate chiefs, factories, and machinery for annual reports. Other areas include scientific, medical, environmental, fashion, and newspaper photography. About one third of photographers are self-employed.

Pilot

Pilots transport passengers and cargo and perform other tasks, such as crop dusting, inspecting power lines, and taking photographs. They monitor and operate electronic instruments in flight and communicate with air traffic controllers. Using information from dispatchers and weather forecasters, they choose a route, an altitude, and a speed. Pilots work for airlines, air taxi companies, and major corporations with their own airplanes. Some work as flight instructors.

Plumber

Plumbers put in and repair the system of pipes, valves, faucets, and other equipment that carries water throughout a structure. They also work on systems that carry steam, air, and other liquids and gases. Most plumbers work for contractors engaged in new construction. Some are self-employed.

Printer

Printers are experts in type composition (setting words into type), photography, platemaking, presswork, and binding. They may specialize in one of the basic types of printing methods—letterpress, lithography, or photogravure. Most printers work for newspapers and commercial printing companies.

Real Estate Agent

Real estate agents must know how to evaluate property and how to assist in the buying and selling of land and structures. They show properties to clients, arrange for financing, and manage ownership documents. They may also manage rental properties and leasing. Most real estate agents work in small real estate firms.

Recording Specialist

The production and recording of sound in the form of records, TV and radio commercials and shows, and movie soundtracks require the talents of recording specialists. These specialists include recording engineering technicians and production assistants. These professionals work with complex production and recording equipment. They must position microphones and make the appropriate adjustments on a studio console. They also need to know how to mix, modulate, monitor, and record sound.

Refrigeration Technician

(see Air-Conditioning Technician)

Respiratory Therapist

Respiratory therapists treat patients with cardiorespiratory conditions and emergencies, such as asthma, emphysema, shock, and heart failure. They use special equipment to help restore normal functioning to the heart-lung system. Most are employed in hospitals. However, some technicians work for oxygen equipment rental companies, ambulance services, and nursing homes.

Retailer

Retailers must both buy and sell goods. (They buy from the wholesaler and sell to the consumer.) They must be experts in choosing and purchasing goods, pricing, financial management, advertising and promotions, and personnel management. Retailers work for large department store chains, where they often specialize in one area of retailing, and for smaller stores. Many are self-employed.

Seaman

(see Marine Technician)

Secretary/Transcriptionist

Secretaries/transcriptionists are responsible for scheduling appointments, screening telephone calls, typing, and transcribing letters and documents. They also process and send information to staff members and to people at outside organizations. Additional duties may include record keeping, preparing letters, and arranging and coordinating special functions. (See also Legal Secretary and Medical Secretary.)

Security Officer

Security officers are responsible for checking security situations and recommending protective devices to minimize loss. They also handle preemployment checks and may be responsible for observing suspects. In retail stores, they attempt to reduce shoplifting, the passing of bad checks, and other illegal practices.

Shorthand Reporter

Shorthand reporters record all statements made during a formal proceeding. Their services are often required to record transactions and the proceedings of meetings, conventions, and other private activities. Almost half of all shorthand reporters work as court reporters. As court reporters, they take down all statements made during a legal process and present their record as the official transcript.

Skin-Care Specialist

Skin-care specialists are skilled in conditioning the skin. They massage, tone, and clean the skin, and they may apply lotions, oils, and creams. They must also be able to examine skin types and conditions before treatment. Skin-care specialists are employed in hairdressing salons, salons in large department stores, and skin-care centers.

Surgical Technician

(see Operating Room Technician)

Surveyor

Surveyors measure construction sites and help determine

(continued)

official land boundaries, assist in deciding land worth, and collect information for maps and charts. They use special instruments to determine the exact location of hills, lines, reference points, and curves in the earth's surface and record the information for consideration in engineering plans. Most surveyors work for construction companies, engineering and architectural consulting firms, and local, state, and federal governments.

Tailor

Tailors measure clients, cut fabric, and sew materials by hand or machine. They must know how to fashion every type of garment, from men's suits to ladies' evening dresses. Tailors also make clothing alterations to improve clothing fit. Most work for small tailoring shops. Many are self-employed.

Television Production Specialist

(see Motion Pictures/Television Production Specialist)

Theater Production Specialist

Attending to the details of scenery, costumes, lighting, props, and choreography requires the talents and skills of theater production specialists. These include business managers, theater managers, technical directors, and production stage managers. Working backstage, these professionals ensure that the show goes on properly.

Tool and Die Designer

Tool and die designers create and develop a design for the machinery and equipment needed to produce manufactured goods. They draw designs for jigs and fixtures, metal forms for molding metal and plastics, gauges, and other tools needed in production. Tool and die designers know about mechanical principles involving tolerance, stress, strain, friction, and vibration. Most work in plants that produce manufacturing, construction, and farm machinery. Others work in auto, aircraft, and other transportation equipment industries; small tool and die shops; and electrical machinery plants.

Transcriptionist

(see Secretary/Transcriptionist)

Travel Specialist

Assisting travelers in making plans and arranging trips requires the services of travel specialists. These specialists include travel agents, reservation clerks, and passenger and ticket agents. These workers are employed by travel agents and transportation companies.

Truck Driver

Truck drivers haul goods over long and short distances. Local drivers move goods from terminals and warehouses to factories, stores, and homes within the area. Long-distance drivers can travel a route for up to several days, covering many miles and crossing state borders. Truck drivers must meet Department of Transportation requirements regarding age (must be over 21), health, vision, hearing, driving record, road skills, and knowledge of federal regulations.

Upholsterer

Upholsterers repair and rebuild upholstered furniture.

(continued)

They understand fabric features and the methods of fabric repair. At various stages, these professionals work on the frame, cover, trim, webbing, padding, and springs. Tools include a tack puller, chisel, and mallet. Upholsterers may need to operate sewing machines.

Veterinary Assistant

Veterinary assistants help prepare animals for examination and surgery. They may sterilize instruments, take samples, administer medication, and perform lab and X-ray tests. In addition, they may be required to make appointments, keep records, and handle billing. Most veterinary assistants work in veterinarians' offices, veterinary hospitals, kennels, research institutes, and zoos.

Vocational Nurse

(see Nurse, Vocational)

Watch Repairer

Watch repairers (frequently called watchmakers) fix broken-down watches and clocks. They take the movement apart and determine the problem. They may have to replace parts or clean and oil the mechanism. Most watch repairers work in jewelry stores. About one third are self-employed.

Welder

Welders are required to know about heat processes and types of metals and joints. They also must know how to read and follow blueprints. Some specialize in ship welding, pipeline welding, and maintenance welding. Most welders are employed in industries that manufacture boilers, bulldozers, trucks, ships, and heavy machinery. Others repair metal products and help construct buildings, bridges, and pipelines.

X-ray Technician

X-ray technicians prepare and position the patient to be X-rayed. They position the X-ray machine and set the controls to achieve the right density, detail, and contrast. X-ray technicians work in physicians' offices and hospitals.

Works Consulted for This Book

Chronicle Occupational Briefs. 5 vols. Moravia, New York: Chronicle Guidance Publications, 1984–88.

Chronicle Vocational School Manual. Moravia, New York: Chronicle Guidance Publications, 1986.

Dencus, Celia. *Career Perspectives: Your Choice of Work.* Belmont, California: Wadsworth, 1972.

Feingold, S. Norman, and Norma Reno Miller. *Emerging Careers: New Occupations for the Year 2000 and Beyond.* Garrett Park, Maryland: Garrett Park Press, 1983.

Gramling, L. G. *Blood, Sweat, and Tears: Calculating Your Career Costs.* New York: Rosen, 1986.

Halacy, Daniel Stephen. *Survival in the World of Work.* New York: Scribner, 1975.

Hebert, Tom, and John Coyne. *Getting Skilled: A Guide to Private Trade and Technical Schools.* 2nd ed. New York: E. P. Dutton, 1980.

Hopke, William E. *The Encyclopedia of Careers and Vocational Guidance.* 6th ed. 3 vols. Chicago: J. G. Ferguson, 1984.

Jones, Clayton. "Career Kit for the '80s." *Christian Science Monitor,* October 23, 1979.

Miller, Roger LeRoy. *Personal Finance Today.* St. Paul: West Publishing, 1979.

Nardone, Thomas. "The Job Outlook in Brief." *Occupational Outlook Quarterly,* Spring 1982, pp. 2–34.

National Association of Trade and Technical Schools. *Handbook 1988 of Private Accredited Trade and Technical Schools: Career Education That Works for America.* Rockville, Maryland: NATTS, 1988.

———. *Trade and Technical Careers and Training, 1986–87.* Rockville, Maryland: NATTS, 1986.

(continued)

Prudential Insurance Company of America. *Facing Facts About Vocational Education for Your Career*. Newark: Prudential, 1975.

Shanahan, William F. *College, Yes or No*. New York: Arco, 1980.

State of Florida Department of Education. *Decisions Ahead*. Tallahassee: Center for Career Development Services, 1985.

——. *Florida Postsecondary Education Information Directory*. Tallahassee: Center for Career Development Services, 1986.

U.S. Department of Labor, Bureau of Labor Statistics. *Employment Projections for 2000*. Washington, D.C.: GPO, 1987.

——. *Occupational Outlook Handbook*. Annual. Washington, D.C.: GPO.

——. *Occupational Projections and Training Data*. Annual. Washington, D.C.: GPO.

Wolf, Harold A. *Personal Finance*. 4th ed. Boston: Allyn, 1975.

About the Authors

Dr. James Myers is the Director of the Regional Services Institute at the University of North Florida in Jacksonville, Florida. He also serves as a consultant and resource person for business and industry. His areas of specialty are prevailing wage rates, labor pools, vendors, locations, and financial assistance for expansion and for start-up operations. Dr. Myers has published numerous articles and books dealing with training, job opportunities, and personnel recruitment.

Elizabeth Werner Scott has earned a master's degree in guidance and counseling and has more than fifteen years of experience in career exploration and employability skills. As Director of the Urban Skills Center in Jacksonville, Florida, Ms. Werner Scott was responsible for the training and job placement of students who enrolled in the center's program.

Both authors have extensive experience and expertise in the planning, development, and implementation of successful career development programs that have been responsible for the placement of thousands of individuals in good jobs with a future.

Getting Skilled, Getting Ahead
is available for purchase at your local bookstore.

Any institution or organization wishing to purchase this book in large quantities (10 or more copies) should contact the publisher directly:

Peterson's
1-800-EDU-DATA
(In NJ, 609-243-9111)
(Monday–Friday, 8:30 a.m.–4:30 p.m. Eastern time)